CACTI

Written by Susan Stephenson
Cacti supplied by Ralph Northcott at Westfield Cacti

KUDOS

Published by Kudos, an imprint of Top That! Publishing plc.
Copyright © 2004 Top That! Publishing plc,
Tide Mill Way, Woodbridge, Suffolk, IP12 IAP,
www.kudosbooks.com
Kudos is a Trademark of Top That! Publishing plc

Contents

Introduction

Cacti are arguably the most intriguing plants on the planet, and the vast array of forms available are a source of continual fascination to both experts and enthusiasts alike.

Cacti come in a huge variety of shapes, forms, colours and textures. Stems can be reddish, grey-green or blue-green. Many specimens have swollen stems, few have leaves in the conventional sense, and they can take various forms from rounded and columnar, to trailing or cristate (close to the ground).

Many species possess wicked spines – sometimes robust, hooked and terribly sharp. Other examples are covered in a downy hair, which can be so dense it masks the stems beneath, giving the plant a bearded appearance. There may be several forms within a single genus (family or group), and many collectors concentrate on just one or two genera.

Cacti can take several years to flower, so are often grown and enjoyed more for their shapes, textures and forms. However, the infrequent flowering of some varieties is its own reward – imagine the satisfaction when a carefully nurtured specimen bursts into bloom after 30 years.

Cacti are great fun to grow, relatively easy to care for, and their longevity and constant ability to impress and surprise makes them ideal house plants.

Most cacti originate from the dry, semi-desert areas of the world. They have adapted to withstand long periods when water is scarce, or even when rainfall is non-existent for several months at a time.

As our understanding of this incredible group of plants increases, more and more species can be successfully grown in cultivation and in the home.

With the basic provision of heat, a suitable growing medium and good light, many species are very easy to grow and make robust plants. They are able to withstand dry conditions and poor soil quality that might harm other groups of plants, and are capable of surviving periods with minimal maintenance.

Like house plants, most cacti are frost tender and do best when kept indoors. However, some are hardy enough to be grown outdoors throughout the year in milder areas.

Cacti respond well to tender, loving care during their growing periods and little or no care during their dormant ones, making them very rewarding to grow.

Natural Habitats of Cacti

Cacti can be broadly divided into two main groups: forest and desert cacti. Both categories originate in the New World (North and South America).

 Desert Cacti

Many desert cacti come from the arid or semi-desert areas of the southwestern United States, and South American countries. These areas are some of the harshest regions of the world and are dry, hot, rocky and very inhospitable. Yet, cacti remain above ground and thrive in these harshest of environments.

Desert cacti are used to bright, sunny conditions and flower after a period of rest. This dormant period occurs when water is in short supply, usually in the hottest, driest part of the year. However, in cultivation desert cacti are more likely to enter a dormant period during the cool winter months.

Most of these cacti are accustomed to stony, or sandy soil and in cultivation, will need a fairly open and gritty compost. They grow best in quickly draining soil and will not tolerate soil that remains saturated.

Naturally, they like plenty of fresh air. They can survive long periods with little or no water (sometimes less than 30 cm a year), and are able to withstand searing heat during the day (in excess of 38°C) and bitter cold at night. Few other groups of plants can survive such dramatic fluctuations in temperature.

Rain often falls in sudden bursts, which is why many desert cacti grow rapidly and flower after a dormant period. Many produce relatively large, luxuriant flowers in vibrant colours. These are often sweetly scented to attract pollinators, and can be long- or short-lived, some opening at night and fading before morning.

☀ Forest Cacti

Although most varieties are considered to be desert cacti, some specimens originate in the forests of tropical South America. They are usually epiphytic (a non-parasitic plant that grows on another) and, with the exception of a few species, are characterised by flattened stems with a leaf-like appearance. These cacti grow in warm areas, with less temperature fluctuation and better water supplies than the desert cacti. Dormant periods vary but, like desert cacti, they flower best after a period of rest. Collectively they are known as forest cacti.

Forest cacti generally prefer a fertile growing medium and are shade tolerant. They often lodge in crevices on trees, or between stones, and grow in the debris that accumulates around them. The environment in which they originated is very different from that of desert cacti, so it is little wonder that they have different forms and requirements.

Unlike the globular, or columnar, desert cacti, forest cacti often have a trailing growth habit. Many forest cacti have glorious flowers, often sweet-smelling, which are large in relation to the size of the plant. This attracts pollinators from the depths of the forest.

Due to the nature of their habitat, forest cacti tolerate a narrower temperature range (13–24°C) and usually thrive in dappled shade. They are used to the humid atmosphere of the forest, so when grown at home they often require misting in dry weather and frequent watering during the flowering period. Also, they are not tolerant of draughty conditions as the air in their natural habitat is relatively still.

Understanding the natural conditions of cacti is an important factor in growing them successfully. Determining whether they are desert or forest cacti is vital to gain an understanding of their likely requirements. Many cacti spend years as house plants, producing little active growth which is largely due to neglect, or the fact they don't have a dormant period. However, once you understand where they come from, it is easier to meet their needs. In return, you will get plants that flourish and produce the kind of growth expected of their species.

Buying and Selecting Plants

Millions of cactus plants are sold every year, many of which become little more than green ornaments if not chosen carefully. Your first consideration should be where to site the plant. With a site in mind, establish whether it is shady or in bright light, humid or dry, constantly warm or cooler at night. Having a better understanding of its origins should now help you select an appropriate species for the site.

When you come to choose the actual plant, a number of things will tell you whether it is a healthy specimen.

The stem should be firm and succulent, not droopy or falling over. There should be no mottling or corky patches on the surface – these can be indications of sudden chilling, insect damage, physical damage, or that the plant has had a sudden shock, such as over- or under-watering.

Check the base of the plant for signs of rot or collapse, which is an indication of basal rot. The stems should not be misshapen or over-elongated as this indicates that the plant has had too much warmth in winter, or too much light. The plant should be sturdy and firmly rooted, showing healthy, strong growth.

Bronze mottling of the stem surface indicates a possible red spider mite infestation, and any shrivelling of the stem tips can be due to soft rot in the tissues below.

In general the cactus should be healthy and unblemished in appearance. It should show new growth or be forming flower buds. It should not be in too small a pot as this makes it difficult to transplant. Make sure there is plenty of room in the pot so that the plant's growth is not restricted. If the cactus is spiny, make sure the spines are growing evenly and are not damaged. If it has fleshy stems, these should be plump and succulent.

Growing Conditions

Cacti are generally very robust plants and grow well providing their basic needs are met. They all need warmth and an open, freely-draining growing medium. Some prefer a slightly alkaline soil, so should be mulched with limestone chippings.

Water

Desert cacti should be watered from late spring until early autumn. During the growth period, watering should be carried out whenever the compost feels dry.

In their natural conditions, water may not fall for months, or even years, but these times of drought end in torrents of water falling in a very short period. Therefore, once watering has begun, it is important that it is maintained in order to encourage growth and flowering.

In late summer, the amount of water should be reduced. Also, to avoid shrivelling of the stems, water should only be given from mid-October if the compost becomes very dry. Cacti grown outdoors will have little requirement for watering unless there is a very long period of drought in the summer months.

For forest cacti, watering should increase after the rest period, just as buds start to form (although this varies from species to species). When flowering, and during active growth, the plants should be watered frequently to stop the compost drying out. Cacti do not like alkaline water so, if your tap water is hard, use rainwater.

Temperature

Desert cacti require warm conditions (13–19°C is ideal, but can be lower depending on the species) from spring to autumn and then a cooler period. Plants kept indoors on windowsills should be brought into the room to avoid a sudden drop in temperature at night. Some species require slightly warmer winter temperatures.

The ideal temperature to keep forest cacti is 13–20°C. During the resting period the temperature can be slightly lower at 13–18°C. Most homes provide temperatures that are acceptable to cacti.

Light and Shade

Getting the light requirements right for cacti can be hard, but desert cacti generally require a sunny spot, especially in winter. If they are grown in a greenhouse, they may need some shading during the hottest months.

Cacti grown outdoors will generally appreciate bright sunlight, but even these may require some temporary shading during a long, hot spell.

Forest cacti need bright light but do not like direct light. Many tolerate dappled shade. Draughts should be avoided for all cacti.

Humidity

Desert cacti will grow well in conditions with low air humidity, but forest cacti need a humid atmosphere, especially during active growth – a daily misting is the best way to provide this.

Feeding

Cacti require feeding during active growth and a standard fertiliser containing a balanced mix of nutrients should be used. Feed once a month and follow the manufacturer's instructions. Apply the mix at half strength for those cacti used to poor soils.

General Maintenance

Cacti are relatively easy to maintain but, like all plants, they do have a few basic needs that should be met.

✳ Growing Media

It can be difficult to decide the best medium in which to grow cacti, but an understanding of the plant's natural habitat can be a great advantage.

Desert cacti thrive in standard cactus compost which is comprised of three-parts loam-based compost or two-parts loamless compost to one-part 6 mm grit. Top dress (adding compost, or similar, to the top of the soil without watering the material into the soil) either with compost mix or a 1 cm layer of grit. Some species prefer alkaline conditions, in which case a top dressing of limestone chippings can be applied instead of grit.

Forest cacti thrive in epiphytic cactus compost which comprises three-parts loam-based compost, or loamless compost, to two-parts 6 mm grit and one-part leaf mould.

If grown outdoors (usually in areas with a minimum of 10°C, except for some fully hardy species) cacti can be planted in containers or raised beds containing a mix of two-parts loamless compost, or coconut fibre or granulated bark, and one-part 6 mm grit. A slow-release balanced fertiliser should be added to the mix for optimum growth. Do not be tempted to use garden soil, builders' sand or grit, or old compost.

✳ Air Humidity

Desert cacti should not be misted in the summer and, apart from Cleistocactus, grow well in relatively low humidity. They may benefit from being placed outside when conditions are warm. Forest cacti, on the other hand, require misting frequently in warm, dry weather.

Feeding

Most cacti grow in conditions where there are rich sources of nutrients available. Sometimes plants show signs of deficiencies which can be due to the soil they are grown in. Often a change of compost will help.

During the active growing period, cacti will benefit from monthly feeds to boost healthy growth and flowering. You can buy proprietary fertilisers, but a general mixture containing all the basic nutrients is sufficient. Apply according to the manufacturer's instructions.

Feeding should be avoided during the dormant period, or when the soil is dry, as this may cause damage to the plant.

Ventilation

Cacti like good ventilation but not draughts, so make sure the plants are in a well-ventilated situation. Extreme heat can be avoided in a greenhouse by using shading or blinds to keep temperatures between 27–30°C. Plants grown outdoors may need temporary shade in very hot periods.

☀ Special Equipment and Tools

Little is required in the way of special tools. A pointed trowel can be handy when loosening soil around a plant before re-potting and, if you are handling a prickly plant, it can be advantageous to wear stout gloves – not rubber ones as the spines will tear them easily.

To avoid handling the spines when lifting prickly specimens, it's a good idea to use a small piece of rubber, or a thick piece of card, just long enough to go around the plant's base.

A mister is useful if you are growing epiphytic cacti, as a sprayed mist of water is the easiest way to raise the air humidity during the growing season.

If you are going away during the growing season you may want to invest in a ceramic water reservoir that you can push down into the soil near the plant. This will release water as the compost dries out.

It is worth noting that cacti can be very heavy plants, especially when they are succulent during the growing periods, so you may want to think about ensuring the place you site your plants is strong enough to support their weight.

☀ Hygiene

Cacti can gather dust between their spines, ribs, or amongst their hairs. During the growing season, gently spray the plants to remove any clinging dirt or dust. If your cacti are outdoors, a light spray from a sprinkler or hose will usually do the trick.

It is advisable to check the growing medium for any signs of fungal growth, as many fungi thrive in the damp, warm conditions that are provided by a watered cactus at its soil level.

☀ Potting and Re-potting

Pots for cacti should always be the correct size and not too large. Re-potting should only be necessary when the plant grows larger, and no more than once a year. Tap the compost around the roots to secure the plant but do not press it down as it needs to retain an open structure.

Re-potted plants should not be watered until a week or two has passed, and the plant should be kept in warm conditions to allow it to settle. Re-potting should be done at the start of the growing season.

Cacti Characteristics

All cacti are members of one family of plants – the Cactacea. They generally have swollen stems packed with water storage tissue, thick cuticles to keep water in, and several have downy hairs to trap moisture as well.

In many cases, the leaves of cactacea have evolved into spines so the surface area from which they can lose water is reduced. The spines also deter grazing animals. In very dry periods, some species even drop their spines in order to conserve valuable moisture.

Cacti are often referred to as stem succulents because their stems are adapted to store water in special tissues, thus resulting in their swollen appearance. The stems often have an additional covering of wool (filaments) for increased protection from water loss. These woolly filaments also help trap any moisture in the air, as water condenses on them during the night. A few cacti possess water storage tissue in their roots.

Cacti are usually geometrical, which is the most efficient shape for water retention, and they often grow in columns or spheres. Their stems are generally green because they have, in most cases, taken over the function of leaves and contain chlorophyll for photosynthesising. Forest cacti, in particular, have flattened stems with broad surfaces to absorb as much light as possible in shaded conditions.

Most cacti have ribs which expand or contract depending on how much water is in the stem. Along the ridges of the ribs form structures unique to cacti, called areoles.

Areoles are the distinguishing feature of all cacti. They are cushion-like growths from which spines, hairs, flowers, leaves and shoots originate, and can be sunken or raised.

Spines are borne as radials where they arise around the edge of an areole, or as centrals arising from the centre of an areole. Water condenses on the spines and drips to the soil around the roots.

While cacti often flourish in poor soil, they rarely do well on pure sand as the fine particles hold very few nutrients.

Most cacti have shallow roots and will adapt easily to being grown in containers. Some epiphytic cacti also produce small radial roots from the stems to absorb moisture from the air.

Certain specimens have a structure called a cephalium, which usually forms at the terminal tip of a stem, stopping further vegetative growth. It is woody and covered in a mass of woolly spines and flowers. In some, the cephalium forms laterally, allowing upward growth to continue, in which case it is called a pseudocephalium. Most cacti are generally small plants and few grow to a height of more than 2.5 m.

The cactacea family is divided into many genera. Each genus has characteristics specific to it and of particular interest. *Echinocereus*, for example, is a genus of varied, small cacti that flower while young; often with very attractive blooms. Most cacti in this genus are very spiny.

By contrast, those of the genus *Astrophytum* have fewer spines and have ribs radiating outwards, giving them their common name of star cacti.

Another genus, *Echinocactus*, are large, globe-shaped, and covered in spines, some of which are dangerously sharp.

Echinopsis are small cacti with barrel-shaped growth and strong ribs. Many of these have showy, heavily-scented flowers. *Mammillaria* are globular or cylindrical, and spiny, with small flowers produced in circles.

Epiphyllum are epiphytic cacti that have large and very showy flowers from April to June. They require a period of rest in December and January with little, or no, watering during this time. In their natural environment, these cacti grow in trees or on rocks – in cultivation, they prefer

some shade in spring and summer, and a compost containing extra leaf mould or peat substitute.

Rhipsalidopsis has flattened, arching stems which carry very attractive flowers in spring. *Schlumbergera* are similar to *Rhipsalidopsis* and bear flowers in shades of pink, magenta, lilac or white. They flower when days are short and nights are long, but artificial lighting may interfere with this.

Some cacti only flower at night. The flowers may be short-lived, opening in the evening and fading by morning so, if flowers are your goal, it is probably best to avoid these specimens which include *Echinopsis eyreisii*, *Cephalocereus senelis* and *Eriocereus bondplantii*.

☀ A Note about Names

Cacti are listed under their Latin names with their common names given where possible. Sometimes, a plant has been re-classified and reassigned to a different group but the plants may still be listed in some directories under their old name(s). This name is the synonym (abbreviated to 'syn.') and is given, where applicable, with the common name of the plant. The abbreviations of 'ssp.' and 'var.' represent 'subspecies' and 'variety' respectively.

Astrophytum myriostigma

Bishop's Mitre

Syn. Echinocactus myriostigma,
Astrophytum prismaticum,
Astrophytum columnare

This is a solitary, spherical or columnar cactus. It has 4–6 very prominent ribs and spineless areoles. Its smooth, grey-green flesh is covered with dense, closely-packed white scales. It has glossy, yellow, sweet-smelling flowers up to 6 cm long and 3 cm wide, which appear as tufts at the top of the stem and bloom throughout the summer. These are followed by a reddish fruit.

Height and Spread

It can reach 60 cm in height and 8 cm in diameter. Some mature plants grow to over 1.2 m high and 20 cm in diameter.

Location and Temperature

It grows best in full sun or light shade. In light shade, it takes on a darker colour. Indoors, it suits a brightly-lit windowsill. It is generally comfortable down to 10°C, but will resist short periods of cold down to a minimum of –6°C.

Growing Medium and Maintenance

Indoors, use proprietary multipurpose compost, or standard cactus compost, with lime chippings added. Outdoors, grow in quickly-draining, poor, slightly alkaline soil (pH 7.5–8.0).

One of the easiest Astrophytum to grow, it should be watered moderately during the growing season, and left dry during winter. If watering continues into autumn when temperatures start to fall, it is susceptible to rot. Check regularly for mealy bugs and root mealy bugs.

Astrophytum ornatum

Monk's Hood
*Syn. Echinocactus ornatus,
Astrophytum glabrescens*

This is a solitary, spherical or columnar cactus. It usually has eight ribs which may be spiralled. The ribs bear closely-packed areoles and spines which can be over 2 cm long. These grow in a pattern of one central and 5–10 radial spines. The flesh is strongly speckled with white, woolly scales. It produces single, pale yellow flowers in summer once it has grown to at least 15 cm tall (which can take up to six years). These flowers can be 2.5 cm across and 10 cm long.

Height and Spread

It can reach 1.2 m in height and 15 cm in diameter, though pot-grown plants are much smaller.

Location and Temperature

Preferring light shade, grow indoors on a windowsill or in a temperate greenhouse where temperatures shouldn't dip below 10°C. Frost tender but can be grown outdoors, in full sun or dappled shade.

Growing Medium and Maintenance

Indoors, use a proprietary multipurpose compost, or standard cactus compost, with crocks at the bottom of the pot for drainage. Outdoors, grow in free-draining, low-fertility, slightly alkaline soil.

In summer, water when the compost feels dry. Do not water in winter. *Astrophytum ornatum* prefers poor soil, so only give fertiliser containing nitrogen (N), potassium (P) and phosphorous (K) at half strength in summer. Feed just before the flowers bloom this should prevent the plant putting on vegetative growth instead of producing flowers.

Cereus peruvianus monstrosus

Rock Cactus

Syn. Cereus hildemannius 'monstrosus'

A glossy blue-green columnar plant, and a mutation of *Cereus peruvianus*, which originates in South America. Cereus normally grow as columnar cacti, but in Rock Cactus the apex divides irregularly giving the plant a distinctly odd appearance. Due to the distortion of the ribs, the thick woolly areoles and spines can stick out at odd angles.

The long, rigid spines are usually in a pattern of 4–7 radials and one or two longer, thicker central spines. Usually they form just a few columns. Large, white, funnel-shaped flowers are borne on older specimens from summer to autumn, and open at night. These are followed by fleshy red, orange or yellow fruit which contain black seeds.

☀ Height and Spread

May reach a height of 1 m and a width of 70 cm.

☀ Location and Temperature

Indoors, grow in full light. Outdoors, grow in full sun. It does well if grown under glass. It is not frost hardy and requires a minimum temperature of 10°C.

☀ Growing Medium and Maintenance

Indoors, grow it in proprietary multipurpose compost or standard cactus compost. Outdoors, it needs very well-drained, poor, humus-rich soil with a slightly acidic pH (5.5–6.5).

Water freely in the growing season but do not mist. Keep it almost dry in winter, never allowing the compost to remain damp. Apply a low-nitrogen liquid fertiliser at four-week intervals during the growing season.

Cleistocactus hyalacanthus

Syn. Cleistocactus jujuyensis,
Cleistocactus straussii var. jujuyensis

A branching, columnar cactus with
grey-green stems, each with 17–25 ribs.
The stems may be up to 6 cm thick.
They are covered with hairy white bristles
which gives them a soft appearance.
The spines are brown-yellow or creamy
white and appear in a pattern of three or
four centrals and 20–30 radials. Pink, or
pale red, flowers are borne along the ribs
in summer and can be 4 cm long.

✳ Height and Spread
Cleistocactus hyalacanthus can grow to
a height of 1 m and with a spread of
over 70 cm.

✳ Location and Temperature
Indoors, it prefers bright light and low
humidity. Outdoors it prefers to be in
full sun. It requires a minimum
temperature of 10ºC.

✳ Growing Medium and Maintenance
Grow in proprietary multipurpose
compost or standard cactus compost.
Outdoors, grow it in low-fertility,
humus-rich, well-drained soil.

Water generously during the summer
but do not mist. Feed with half-strength
balanced (N, P and K) liquid fertiliser
every 5–6 weeks. Keep dry between
autumn and spring.

Cleistocactus winteri cristate

Golden Rat Tail

*Syn. Borzicactus aureispinus,
Cleistocactus aureispinus*

Cleistocactus winteri is freely branching
and normally forms masses of columns.
Its stems are mid-green, up to 6 cm in
diameter, and have 15–17 ribs. Its spines
are golden yellow, giving the stems the
appearance of rats' tails – hence its
common name. In the mutant cristate
form (pictured), the stems grow in crests
and the plant is much more compact. The
areoles are creamy yellow and bear about
fifty spines, each up to 1 cm long. Kept
under optimum conditions, this cactus
bears many pink flowers which can be up
to 6 cm long and 5 cm wide. They are
followed by green fruit 1 cm in length.

✳ Height and Spread

It grows up to 90 cm in height with a
spread of 1 m or more.

✳ Location and Temperature

Indoors, grow it in good light and low
humidity. Outdoors, grow it in full sun,
with light shade in very hot periods. It
needs a minimum average temperature
of 10°C and will tolerate frost to –2°C
for very short periods.

✳ Growing Medium and Maintenance

Indoors, grow in proprietary
multipurpose, or standard cactus
compost. Outdoors, grow in poor,
humus-rich, freely-draining soil. Water
well during the growing season and keep
it dry in winter. Apply a half-strength,
balanced liquid fertiliser every
5–6 weeks.

Coryphantha cornifera

Rhinoceros Cactus
Syn. Mammillaria cornifera,
Coryphantha radians,
Coryphantha schwartziana

A striking, solitary perennial cactus.
The tubercles are angular and each one
has an areole bearing 1–3 central and
7–12 radial spines. The plant has a
woolly centre at the top of its head.
Yellow flowers are borne in summer and
may be up to 6 cm in diameter. Mature
plants form a columnar shape.

Height and Spread

It can reach a height of 12 cm and
a spread of 15 cm.

Location and Temperature

Coryphantha cornifera will grow in full
sun, but some light shade is needed
during very hot periods. Remove it from a
windowsill during prolonged hot periods
to prevent scorching. It prefers sun if kept
outdoors. It is hardy to –5°C for short
periods but prefers a minimum average
temperature of 10°C.

Growing Medium and Maintenance

In containers, grow it in proprietary
soil-less, multipurpose compost or
standard cactus compost. Outdoors,
grow in poor, humus-rich, gritty,
well-drained soil.

Water sparingly in summer and keep dry
in winter. Apply low nitrogen liquid
fertiliser monthly during the growing
season. Outside, mix a little balanced,
slow-release fertiliser into the soil. Good
drainage is essential.

Coryphantha elephantidens

Elephant's Tooth

Syn. Coryphantha sulcolanata,
Echinocactus elephantidens,
Coryphantha greenwoodii

Coryphantha elephantidens is a
clumping, globular cactus with slightly
flattened, spherical stems. Each head may
be up to 15 cm in diameter. The rounded
tubercles may be up to 4 cm long and
2.5 cm wide. They are velvety to touch,
deeply grooved and arranged in thirteen
rows. It has woolly tubercle axils and
white wool is present on the crown.

The solitary, funnel-shaped flowers are
scented, deep pink with darker centres,
and appear in summer. They may be
10 cm across, which is large for the
size of the plant. They are followed by
cylindrical green fruit containing oval,
or kidney-shaped, brown seeds.

☀ Height and Spread

It grows to 15 cm in height
with a diameter up to 20 cm.

☀ Location and Temperature

Coryphantha elephantidens will grow in
full sun or light shade. It is usually grown
indoors but can survive outdoors in a
warm, arid garden with full sun. If grown
in pots, make sure there are plenty of
crocks at the bottom to allow free drainage.
It is hardy, withstanding temperatures down
to –3°C for short periods, but prefers an
average temperature of 12°C.

☀ Growing Medium and Maintenance

Indoors, grow it in proprietary
multipurpose compost or standard cactus
compost. A 2 cm-thick layer of grit on the
top will enable water to drain away from
the head. Outside, grow in poor,
humus-rich, gritty, well-drained soil.

Water sparingly, and keep dry in winter.
Give it a low nitrogen feed at four- to
six-week intervals.

The Easter and Christmas Cacti

Rhipsalidopsis have now been incorporated into the genus *Hatiora*, but most people still know them as Easter cacti. They are among the most beautiful of all epiphytic, forest cacti, and flower in April and May. They are simple to grow, and easily root from single or double stem segments. Two species exist – *Rhipsalidopsis gaetneri*, the common Easter cactus which has large orange flowers that only open in sunlight, and the smaller, *Rhipsalidopsis rosea* (now *Hatiora rosea*, see pages 70–71) which has masses of pink flowers. There are white-flowered forms, including *Rhipsalidopsis 'Sirius'*, and many hybrids.

There are six species of *Schlumbergera* and many cultivars. They are commonly known as Christmas cacti (which are also forest cacti) and grown largely for their form and their glorious, tubular flowers. They can still be found listed under the name *Zygocactus*. These plants are also epiphytic and can be grown as epiphytes indoors on wood stems, but are usually grown in pots.

Easter cacti are sometimes confused with Christmas cacti because of their similar habits. There are, however, differences in the flowers – the flowers of Christmas cacti are long and tubular (naturally pollinated by humming birds), while Easter cacti have simple, star-like flowers with no pollen tubes.

See pages 70–71 and 110–111 for more detailed examples of Easter and Christmas cacti.

Echinocactus grusonii

**Mother-in-law's Chair,
Golden Barrel Cactus**

This is a spherical cactus that will elongate and become cylindrical when mature. It is slow growing and has bright, green stems with 20–40 sharply angled ribs. The areoles are yellow and bear golden yellow spines in the pattern of 3–5 centrals and 8–10 radials. The areoles form a dense woolly crown and it is from here that the small, bell-shaped, bright yellow flowers are borne in summer. They can be 6 cm in length but tend to be hidden in the wool of the crown.

Echinocactus grusonii originates in Mexico where it is endangered in the wild. It is popular as a landscaping plant in southwest America, as its golden spines look attractive for many years. The rib structure is not apparent in young plants which have pronounced tubercles until they mature. Only mature specimens flower.

✳ Height and Spread
Indoors, Mother-in-law's Chair can reach a height of 90 cm and a spread of 90 cm. Outside, in warm climates, it can reach 2 m high and wide.

✳ Location and Temperature
Indoors, it likes bright light away from draughts. Outdoors, it thrives in full sun. It needs an average temperature of 12°C but is hardy to –10°C for short periods.

✳ Growing Medium and Maintenance
Indoors, grow it in multipurpose or standard cactus compost. Outdoors, grow in fertile, well-drained soil.

Water often in the growing season but do not let the compost remain damp. Apply half-strength balanced fertiliser at four-week intervals. Keep it dry during the winter dormant season.

Echinocactus platycanthus fa. grandis

Giant Barrel Cactus
Syn. Echinocactus grandis

This is a barrel-shaped cactus with green-grey stems and 18–25 pronounced ribs in mature plants. The areoles are evenly spaced and bear silver-grey spines arranged in a pattern of 1–2 centrals and 7–9 radials. The spines can be up to 2 cm long. It can be grown outside in warmer climates but needs to be at least 10 cm in diameter to thrive. The golden yellow flowers, up to 5 cm in length, are borne in summer and appear in rings at the woolly crown.

✳ Height and Spread

Echinocactus platycanthus slowly grows to 1.5 m in height with a spread of up to 1.2 m.

✳ Location and Temperature

Indoors, it will grow in bright, airy places, such as a conservatory or well-lit windowsill. Outdoors, grow it in full sun. Hardy to –6°C for short periods, it needs a minimum average temperature of 12°C.

✳ Growing Medium and Maintenance

Indoors, grow it in standard cactus compost. Outdoors, it requires free-draining soil.

Giant Barrel Cactus is generally drought resistant so can survive with little water, but regular watering in the growing season will make it grow faster. Keep it dry in winter.

Echinocereus brandegeei

Strawberry Cactus, Casa de Ratas
Syn. Cereus brandegeei,
Echinocereus mamillatus,
Cereus sanborngianus

An upright, or ground-hugging, clump-forming cactus with cylindrical, pale green stems which have 8–10 ribs. Its stems are divided into warty tubercles and may be up to 7 cm thick. Areoles are yellow-green and bear yellow spines with red spots which turn grey as the plant matures.

It has 1–4 central spines which may be up to 3 cm long (the longer ones being flattened), and 10–18 radial, spreading spines. Bell-shaped, pale pink flowers with dark red throats are produced in summer and can be 10 cm long and 4 cm across. These are followed by red, plump, spiny fruit up to 3 cm in diameter.

☀ Height and Spread
Echinocereus brandegeei can reach 1 m in height with a spread of up to 2 m.

☀ Location and Temperature
Grow it indoors in bright light – it will tolerate full sun. In cooler areas, grow it on a bright windowsill, or in a cool or temperate greenhouse with some shade available for hot days. Outdoors, it can be grown in full sun in a desert garden. Hardy to −2°C, it needs an average minimum temperature of 10°C.

☀ Growing Medium and Maintenance
Grow indoors or under glass in proprietary multipurpose, soilless, or standard cactus, compost. Outdoors, grow in free-draining soil.

Water frequently from mid-spring to early autumn and keep completely dry in winter. Strawberry Cactus is prone to rot, so the compost must be dry in the dormant season. During the growing season, apply half-strength balanced liquid fertiliser monthly.

Echinocereus rigidissimus ssp. rubispinus

*Syn. Echinocereus rigidissimus
var. rubispinus*

Usually a solitary, upright cactus with mid-green stems which sometimes branch. The stems can be up to 8 cm in diameter with 12–20 ribs. The mid-green areoles bear reddish-pink spines. The spines are arranged in a pattern of three short centrals and up to thirty radials. Magenta or yellow flowers bloom in summer. They may be up to 7 cm across and have white centres.

☀ Height and Spread
It grows up to 20 cm in height and solitary stems have a width of up to 5 cm.

☀ Location and Temperature
Grow it indoors in bright light. *Echinocereus rigidissimus* will tolerate full sun and needs low humidity. In cool climates, grow on a bright windowsill or in a temperate greenhouse. Outdoors, it can be grown in full sun. It will tolerate slight frost, but needs an minimum average temperature of 10ºC.

☀ Growing Medium and Maintenance
Indoors, or under glass, grow it in proprietary multipurpose compost, or standard cactus compost. Add a layer of grit to the top to keep water away from the stems. Outdoors, grow in free-draining, humus-rich soil. Water frequently from mid-spring to early autumn and keep dry in winter. Prone to rot so keep it dry in the dormant season. During the growing season it will benefit from an application of half-strength balanced liquid fertiliser.

Echinocereus scheeri ssp. gentryi

Hedgehog Cactus
*Syn. Echinocereus salm-dyckianus,
Echinocereus gentryi*

An unusual looking and intriguing plant.
It is a clump-forming, columnar cactus
with yellow-green stems reaching 4 cm in
diameter. The stems have 7–9 ribs. Young
areoles have yellowish felt on them and
are scattered 5–8 mm apart along the
ribs. Its spines are long and sharp in a
pattern of one central and 8–9 radial. The
radials may have reddish tips. Spination
can vary a great deal in this species. The
flowers, which are borne in summer, are
spiny and pink with paler throats.

☀ Height and Spread
Echinocereus scheeri can grow up to
70 cm in height with a spread of up
to 50 cm.

☀ Location and Temperature
It enjoys full sun but will tolerate light
shade. In temperate climates, grow
on a bright windowsill or in a cool
greenhouse. Outdoors, it can be grown
in full sun. It will tolerate a little frost but
needs an minimum average temperature
of 10ºC.

☀ Growing Medium and Maintenance
Indoors, or under glass, grow it in
standard cactus compost. Outdoors,
it needs free-draining soil.

Water infrequently during the growing
season and keep it completely dry in
winter. During the growing season
Echinocereus scheeri will benefit from
an application of half-strength balanced
liquid fertiliser.

Echinopsis aurea

Golden Easter Cactus
*Syn. Lobivia aurea, Pseudolobivia aurea,
Lobivia ancastii, Echinopsis fallax*

A solitary, or clustering, cactus with
grey-green, spherical, thick stems bearing
14–15 ribs. The ribs bear many areoles
from which grow a pattern of four central
spines, 2–3 cm in length, and 8–10 radial
spines of up to 1 cm in length. The large,
trumpet-shaped flowers are produced in
summer, usually from the end of stems.
The flowers are golden yellow in colour,
or sometimes white, pink or red and open
up to 8 cm in diameter.

☀ Height and Spread

Echinopsis aurea can reach 15 cm in
height and over 10 cm in diameter. It
requires a minimum average temperature
of 5°C but prefers temperatures around
10°C. It is frost tender.

☀ Location and Temperature

Grow *Echinopsis aurea* in a shallow pot
as it is susceptible to rot. In areas that are
frost prone, grow it indoors or in a
temperate or warm greenhouse. It
requires bright sunlight to grow well, so
suits a well-lit windowsill. In warmer
climates it can be grown outdoors.

☀ Growing Medium and Maintenance

Indoors, grow it in proprietary soilless
multipurpose or standard cactus compost.
Outdoors, it enjoys full sun or light shade
and soil with excellent drainage.

Water it freely during the growing period.
Apply a nitrogen and potassium-based
fertiliser at monthly intervals to
encourage flowering. Keep it dry
during the winter months.

53

Echinopsis bruchii

South American Barrel Cactus
Syn. Lovibia grandis,
Echinopsis ingens, Lobivia bruchii

A solitary, globular, very spiny cactus
with dark olive-green flesh. Pronounced
ribs vary in number from 20–50. The
areoles are brownish white and bear
four central spines up to 2 cm in length,
and 9–14 radial spines, all of which are
well defined. The striking flowers are
produced in summer and are deep
orange to red in colour and up to
5 cm in diameter.

☀ Height and Spread
Echinopsis bruchii can reach up to 50 cm
in both height and spread.

☀ Location and Temperature
Indoors, it prefers bright, but not direct
light. It makes a good house plant but
will also thrive in a warm, or temperate,
greenhouse. Outdoors, grow it in full sun.
It suits a desert garden but will not
tolerate frost, requiring an minimum
average temperature of 10°C.

☀ Growing Medium and Maintenance
Indoors, grow it in proprietary
multipurpose or standard cactus compost.
Outdoors, grow it in well-drained soil.

Water it frequently in the growing
season and apply a potassium and
nitrogen-based fertiliser once a month,
but do not allow the compost to remain
damp. Keep the compost totally dry
in winter and ensure drainage is
always good.

Echinopsis maximiliana

Syn. Lobivia maximiliana,
Lobivia corbula, Lobivia westii,
Echinopsis caespitosa

A mat-forming cactus with flattened
spherical, oval, or cylindrical pale green
stems that take on a brownish tinge as
the plant matures. The stems can be up to
5 cm in diameter and 20 cm in length.
They have 12–20 ribs divided by cross
furrows to form distinctive tubercles.
White areoles bear light brown spines in
a pattern of one central, curved spine and
4–12 radial spines. This cactus produces
bright red flowers, up to 8 cm long,
with orange-yellow throats and darker
lines inside.

❋ Height and Spread

It grows to 10 cm in height and 5 cm wide,
but seems larger when it forms clusters.

❋ Location and Temperature

Indoors, grow it in bright light with some
direct sunlight. Outdoors, grow it in full
sun or afternoon shade. It prefers an
average minimum temperature of 10°C
and is not tolerant of frost.

❋ Growing Medium and Maintenance

Indoors, grow *Echinopsis maximiliana* in
standard cactus compost or proprietary
soil-based multipurpose compost.
Outside, grow it in free-draining soil.

It needs little water but drainage must
always be maintained. Feed it with
potassium and nitrogen-based liquid
fertiliser every 4–5 weeks.

Echinopsis pachanoi

San Pedro Cactus
Syn. Cereus pachanoi,
Trichocereus pachanoi

A large, columnar, branching cactus originating in the mountainous (1500–2700 m) regions of Ecuador and Peru. It is a striking plant with deeply ribbed, blue-green stems and white flowers up to 22 cm in diameter, which open at night. It has a history of use by native people for the small quantities of mescaline – a hallucinogenic drug – contained in its stems.

✳ Height and Spread
It can grow up to 6 m tall with a spread of 1.8 m.

✳ Location and Temperature
Due to its large size, this cactus is not often grown indoors but will grow outdoors in areas where there is little chance of sharp frosts (minimum temperature of 1°C). It can make a stunning addition to a desert garden and prefers full sun with some light shade. It also grows well in a container placed in a cool greenhouse.

✳ Growing Medium and Maintenance
Grow it in well-drained, gritty, moderately fertile soil with slow-release fertiliser added. It requires little water once established. If kept in a greenhouse, add a little potassium and nitrogen-based fertiliser monthly. If it's slow to grow outdoors, add fertiliser to the soil.

Epiphyllum crenatum var. kimnachii

Orchid Cactus

An upright forest cactus with a cylindrical main stem and grey-green flesh. The main stem branches into flattened smaller stems up to 10 cm across, which give a leaf-like appearance. It bears glorious, funnel-shaped, yellow or pale, creamy-white flowers with green, pink or pale yellow outer petals.

✳ Height and Spread

Orchid Cactus can reach lengths of 3 m with a 3 m spread. Being semi-epiphytic, it grows on trees or in crevices in rocks. The stems develop a trailing habit.

✳ Location and Temperature

Like all Epiphyllum, Orchid Cactus likes a bright, well-lit place and its trailing leaf-like stems habit makes it an attractive container plant. It likes a humid atmosphere so suits a conservatory. Outdoors, it can be grown in free-draining, fertile soil. It likes dappled or partial shade and requires a temperature of 10–15°C. It will not tolerate frost.

✳ Growing Medium and Maintenance

Indoors, grow it in proprietary soil-based, or epiphytic, compost. Outdoors, it thrives in well-drained, fertile soil with added leaf mould.

Keep the atmosphere humid, mist the plant daily, and water it freely during the growing season. To encourage flowering, apply a high potash fertiliser every two weeks from spring to late summer. Its growing medium should be moist, yet free-draining.

Ferocactus emoryi

Coville's Barrel Cactus
Syn. Ferocactus covillei

This is a striking, solitary, large cactus with grey-green flesh and 15–30 very marked ribs. The areoles are widely spaced (2–2.5 cm apart), oval and are covered with brown wool. They bear long, curved spines in a pattern of one 4–10 cm central spine (which may be flattened and is often hooked) and 7–9 white, or reddish, radial spines which may be up to 6 cm long. The funnel-shaped flowers are red and may be up to 7 cm long and 7 cm across. They are followed by an oblong fruit.

✷ Height and Spread
Ferocactus emoryi can reach a height of 2.5 m with a 1 m diameter.

✷ Location and Temperature
Indoors, it can be grown in a conservatory, temperate greenhouse, or another warm but airy location which has free air movement to avoid humidity. Outdoors, it requires full sun and would suit a desert garden. It requires an average minimum temperature of 10ºC but will tolerate short periods of colder conditions.

✷ Growing Medium and Maintenance
Indoors, grow *Ferocactus emoryi* in a container of standard cactus compost. Outdoors, it requires low-fertility, freely-draining soil and some protection from excessive rain.

It needs little water once established and the root area should be kept dry. Keep it dry during the dormant season.

Ferocactus townsendianus

Barrel Cactus

*Syn. Ferocactus peninsulae
var. townsendianus*

A spherical or columnar, fat, globular, solitary perennial cactus with a flattened top. The areoles are evenly spaced along the prominent ribs and bear hooked spines. The flowers are single and are borne between late summer and early autumn. They are funnel-shaped and pale yellow to deep orange in colour originating close to the crown. They are followed by plump, oval-shaped fruit.

❋ Height and Spread

It will grow up to 20 cm tall and with a diameter of 30 cm.

❋ Location and Temperature

Indoors, the Barrel Cactus requires a bright light and suits a well-lit windowsill. Outdoors, where temperatures do not regularly dip below 10°C, it can be grown in full sun. It needs an airy location with low humidity and a minimum, average temperature of 10°C. It will stand a little frost for short periods.

❋ Growing Medium and Maintenance

Grow in proprietary multipurpose or standard cactus compost in pots indoors. Outdoors, it requires low-fertility, freely-draining soil. It may need protection from rain if there is a prolonged wet period.

Keep water away from the root area as it is prone to rot – this type of cactus requires very little water once established. Keep it dry in winter, except on very warm days when it should be misted. Apply a balanced fertiliser at four-week intervals during the growing season.

Gymnocalycium monvillei

Syn. Gymnocalycium multiflorum, Echinocactus ourselianus

This is a cylindrical cactus, which forms clumps when mature. It has bright bluish-green fleshy stems. The flattened yellow spines are spreading, sharp and curved. Its ribs are prominent and it has divided, prominent, warty tubercles. The funnel-shaped, delicate pink to white flowers are borne in summer.

☀ Height and Spread

It can grow to 10 cm in height with a diameter of 22 cm.

☀ Location and Temperature

Indoors, grow it in well-lit conditions but with some shade from hot sunlight. Outside, it prefers light shade in a desert garden. It will tolerate some frost to –8°C for short periods, but prefers a minimum average temperature of 10°C.

☀ Growing Medium and Maintenance

Indoors, grow it in proprietary multipurpose compost with an open structure or standard cactus compost. Outdoors, grow it in low-fertility, well-drained soil with a grit mulch.

Water this cactus regularly in summer and keep it dry in winter. Apply a low nitrogen liquid fertiliser every four weeks during the growing period. It needs to reach 5–8 cm in diameter before it will flower.

Gymnocalycium monvillei ssp. horridispinum

Chin Cactus

Syn. Gymnocalycium horridispinum

This is a globular cactus with fleshy stems, prominent, rounded ribs and diagonal grooves. Areoles bear long, stout, very striking spines which are slightly curved. Large, pink and white funnel-shaped flowers are produced in early summer from the crowns or side areoles. The flowers buds have no hairs or spines (the name of this plant comes from the Greek for 'naked calyx'). The flowers remain open for up to seven days.

☀ Height and Spread

It will grow to reach 20 cm in height with a similar sized spread.

☀ Location and Temperature

The Chin Cactus likes bright light, but shade it from hot sun. Outdoors, grow it in light shade. It needs a minimum average temperature of 10°C and is not frost tolerant.

☀ Growing Medium and Maintenance

Indoors, grow it in proprietary multipurpose or standard cactus compost. Outdoors, grow it in well-drained, poor, gritty soil.

With a summer growing season, water regularly in spring and summer but keep it dry in winter. Apply a low nitrogen liquid feed every four weeks.

Hatiora rosea

Pink-flowered Easter Cactus
Syn. Rhipsalis rosea,
Rhipsalidopsis rosea

A shrubby, hanging forest cactus with flat, slightly angular, jointed stems divided into 3–5 segments, each up to 4 cm long and 10 cm across. The margins are thin and red with minute areoles at the apex of each segment. The segments bear a few hairy, brown bristles. In early spring, it produces a mass of trumpet-shaped, deep-pink flowers up to 3.5 cm across.

✳ Height and Spread

Hatiora rosea grows up to 15 cm in height and spread.

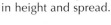

✳ Location and Temperature

Grow in a greenhouse, or on a warm windowsill, with high humidity. Avoid direct sunlight. It suits a hanging basket or container due to its trailing nature. Outdoors, grow in a container on a patio in light shade, avoiding direct sunlight. It is not really suitable for a desert garden. This is not a frost-hardy cactus and requires a minimum temperature of 12°C.

✳ Growing Medium and Maintenance

Grow as epiphytes in epiphytic compost or in standard proprietary, loam-based compost with sterile leaf mould added. Outdoors, grow it in poor, freely-draining, humus-rich, slightly acidic soil with added leaf mould.

Water when growing and mist daily with soft water. Apply half-strength, low-nitrogen liquid fertiliser each month. This cactus needs good drainage. It requires a resting period from October to January when the growing medium should be kept moist, but never over-wet. In February, when flower buds form, increase the temperature and water more frequently.

Hatiora salicornioides

Drunkard's Dream, Spice Cactus
Syn. Hatiora bambusoides,
Rhipsalis stricta, Hariota villigera

A bushy, branching, upright-to-pendant
forest cactus. The stems are long and
divided into club-shaped segments, each
segment being 1–5 cm long and arranged
in whorls. Small, yellow or orange
funnel-shaped flowers bloom in spring
and form on the areoles of new growth.
They are 1 cm long and are followed
by small, yellow fruit.

☀ Height and Spread

The hanging stems of mature
plants grow up to
45 cm long.

☀ Location and Temperature

Indoors, Drunkard's Dream prefers bright
but filtered or indirect light and high
humidity. It suits a hanging basket as it
produces trailing growth. In cool climates,
grow it in a warm greenhouse or
conservatory. Outdoors, it will tolerate
some full sun but prefers light shade. It is
ideally suited to containers on patios but
is not frost tolerant so requires a minimum
temperature of 12°C.

☀ Growing Medium and Maintenance

Grow indoors as an epiphyte or in
epiphytic compost. Outdoors, grow it in
poor, humus-rich, well-drained soil with
an acidic to neutral pH.

It needs little water, except when the air
becomes very dry. In the growing season,
mist it daily. Apply a monthly feed of
half-strength, low-nitrogen liquid fertiliser.
Keep it just moist until flower buds
develop, then increase watering a little to
encourage blooming. Drunkard's Dream
is prone to rot if kept cold and wet,
but can also die back if the soil
becomes too dry.

Leuchtenbergia principis

Agave Cactus

This cactus grows in an angular rosette shape, and is usually solitary or slowly offsetting. The stems are short and cylindrical with woolly axils.
Bluish-green, elongated tubercles of 10–15 cm cover the stems. Large, grey areoles at the tip of the tubercles bear raffia-like spines – usually 1–2 central spines up to 10 cm long, and 8–14 radials up to 5 cm long.

The tubercles open to increase photosynthesis in good conditions, and close to conserve water in dry periods. A tubercle at the apex of the plant bears funnel-shaped, silky, bright yellow flowers up to 8 cm across from summer to autumn.

※ Height and Spread

Grows to a height of 75 cm and a spread of 40 cm.

※ Location and Temperature

Indoors, grow it in full light. It needs a deep pot as it develops a strong, cylindrical tap root when mature. It is well suited to a warm greenhouse. Outdoors, grow it in full sun to light shade. It will tolerate short periods of frost down to –7°C but requires an average temperature of 10°C.

※ Growing Medium and Maintenance

Indoors, grow it in proprietary multipurpose compost, or standard cactus compost, with lime chippings added. Grow outdoors in fairly fertile, sharply draining alkaline soil.

Water carefully – a lack of water will turn the top of the tubercles yellow, whereas too much water will make it rot. Water moderately from spring to late summer, giving a balanced liquid fertiliser every six weeks. Keep it dry from mid-autumn to late spring.

Lophophora williamsii

Peyote Cactus

*Syn. Anhalonium williamsii,
Lophophora lewinii*

A solitary or clump-forming, button-like
cactus that can grow in large groups,
making it very unusual. It has dark,
blue-green stems which are 5–8 cm thick.
Young plants look like swollen green
pebbles as the areoles and ribs are not
pronounced. As they mature, the tubercles
become prominent and the rounded
areoles lose the few weak spines they had
when young and grow grey-white wool
instead. *Lophophora* comes from the
Greek meaning 'crest bearer', referring to
these tufts of wool.

Each stem has 5–13 low ribs and is deeply
furrowed. Its glaucous form gives it its
other common name – the Dumpling
Cactus. The top of the stem is woolly. The
solitary, bell-shaped, bright red or pink
flowers, reach up to 2.5 cm across and
appear at the crown from spring to
autumn, lasting 2–3 days.

Possession of this cactus is illegal in some
countries as it is a source of mescaline, a
mind-altering alkaloid.

Height and Spread

Lophophora williamsii grows 6 cm high
and up to 12 cm wide.

Location and Temperature

In cold climates, grow this cactus in full
light indoors or in a warm greenhouse.
Outdoors, where the climate stays above
10°C, grow it in free-draining, fairly poor,
alkaline soil. It prefers sloping ground in
full sun. It needs a minimum average
temperature of 8°C and is not frost hardy.

Growing Medium and Maintenance

Indoors, grow it in proprietary
multipurpose or cactus compost with
added grit and limestone chippings.
Outside, grow it in well-drained, fairly
poor, alkaline soil.

Water from spring to summer, giving
liquid fertiliser every six weeks.

Mammillaria camptotricha

Bird's Nest Cactus
Syn. Dolichothele camptotricha

A clump-forming cactus with long tubercles, often forming dense clusters. The stems can be up to 7 cm thick and the nipple-like areoles, which give the genus its name (*Mammillaria* comes from the Latin for 'nipple'), bear 2–8 pale green, radial spines. White, sweet-smelling flowers bloom in rings and can be up to 3 cm long. They are borne not from areoles but from the junction of two tubercles. They bloom from summer to autumn, and are followed by long, green fruit that can be mistaken for tubercles.

☀ Height and Spread

Bird's Nest Cactus grows to 8 cm high with a diameter of up to 25 cm.

☀ Location and Temperature

Indoors, grow it in bright light and low humidity, but shade it from very hot sun. Grow it in a shallow pot as it is prone to rot. Outdoors, grow it in full sun. The minimum average growing temperature is 7°C.

☀ Growing Medium and Maintenance

Indoors, grow *Mammillaria camptotricha* in standard cactus compost or proprietary multipurpose compost with added grit. Outdoors, grow it in fairly fertile, freely-draining, gritty soil. Protect it from rain.

Water this cactus often in summer but do not let the compost or soil remain damp. Apply a balanced liquid fertiliser feed every four weeks during the growing period. Keep the compost almost dry in winter. Flowers form from a ring on the previous season's growth so it is important to feed and water this cactus regularly during the growing period.

Mammillaria elongata

Gold Lace Cactus, Lady Finger Cactus

This clustering cactus has thin, delicate-looking, columnar stems with variable spination. The stems are light to mid-green and up to 3 cm thick. The densely-packed areoles bear spines that are light golden-yellow to brown-red in colour, in a pattern of 1–3 central spines and 15–20 radials, although the central spines may be absent. Gorgeous creamy flowers, sometimes with a pink stripe, bloom in summer and are 1–2 cm long.

✳ Height and Spread
Mammillaria elongata grows up to 15 cm high with a diameter up to 35 cm.

✳ Location and Temperature
Indoors, grow it in a bright, airy place with low humidity. Avoid direct sun in the hottest periods. Outdoors, grow it in full sun or light shade. It requires a minimum average temperature of 10°C and does not tolerate frost.

✳ Growing Medium and Maintenance
Indoors, grow Gold Lace Cactus in proprietary multipurpose or standard cactus compost with added grit. Grow it in a shallow pot with a layer of grit on top of the compost. Grow it outdoors in well-drained, fertile soil with added grit for good drainage.

This cactus is prone to rot, so water sparingly during the growing season and ensure drainage is always good. Feed with a balanced liquid fertiliser at four-weekly intervals during the growing season.

Mammillaria geminispina cristate

Twin Spined Cactus, Whitey

This fascinatingly beautiful cristate form of *Mammillaria geminispina* is actually caused by a deformity in the genes, damage to the growing point or infection. The stems are mid-green and grow in undulating waves rather than the usual spherical or columnar form of *Mammillaria geminispina*. The areoles are white and woolly, growing in curved lines along the stem, and bear 2–4 long, brown centrals and 16–20 radials.

☀ Height and Spread

The cristate can form mounds up to 2 m in diameter with each head being up to 18 cm long and 8 cm thick, though it tends to form thicker stems.

☀ Location and Temperature

Indoors, grow it in bright sun and low humidity. Outdoors, it can be grown in full sun. It needs a minimum temperature of 7°C, and is not frost hardy.

☀ Growing Medium and Maintenance

Indoors, grow it in proprietary multipurpose soil-based compost or standard cactus compost. Outdoors, grow it in freely-draining soil with added grit.

Remove any normal growth to maintain the plant's deformity and to stop it reverting to its regular form. Water it during the growing season but keep it dry during winter.

Mammillaria plumosa

Feather Cactus

This clump-forming cactus is stunning to look at. The often hidden stems are mid-green, spherical, and up to 7 cm thick. The areoles bear no central spines but up to forty feathery white radials which can make the body appear to be almost invisible. The white to yellow flowers are few in number and are produced from mid-winter to spring. These are followed by rose-to purple-coloured fruit.

✳ Height and Spread

Feather Cactus grows up to 15 cm high. Its diameter varies but it can form a large mound up to 40 cm across with a head of up to 7 cm wide.

✳ Location and Temperature

Indoors, grow it in a brightly-lit place. Some shade from very hot, direct sun is advisable. Outdoors, grow it in full sun. The minimum temperature should be 7°C. This cactus is not frost hardy.

✳ Growing Medium and Maintenance

Indoors, grow it in shallow pots in proprietary multipurpose or standard cactus compost with an open structure and added grit. Grow in shallow pots. Outdoors, grow it in freely-draining, moderately fertile soil.

Water enough to keep the compost just moist in the growing season. Give a balanced liquid fertiliser feed at four-weekly intervals. This cactus must be kept dry in winter.

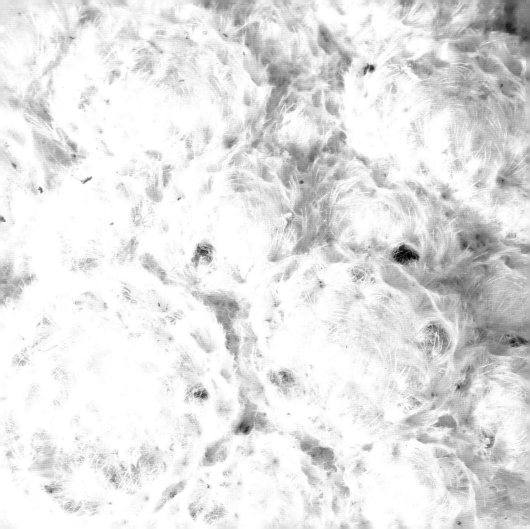

Mammillaria senilis

Syn. *Mamillopsis senilis,
Cochemiea senilis,
Mammillaria digueitti*

A very attractive, rounded,
slowly-clumping cactus with
grey-green stems. The areoles are white
and fluffy. They bear white to grey spines,
some of which are hooked, and long
hairs which give the plant a deceptively
soft appearance. Beautiful, bright red
flowers, up to 5 cm in length and
diameter, are borne near the crowns
from summer to autumn.

✳ Height and Spread
Mammillaria senilis grows up
to 15 cm in height with
a diameter of 10 cm.

✳ Location and Temperature
Indoors, grow it in bright light and low
humidity, with protection from very hot
sun. Grow in a shallow pot with extra
crocks to allow good drainage. Outdoors,
grow it in full sun, or light shade, in a site
with good drainage – a slope is good.
This cactus requires a minimum
temperature of 10°C.

✳ Growing Medium and Maintenance
Indoors, grow it in proprietary
multipurpose or standard cactus compost
with added grit. Outdoors, grow it in
well-drained, fertile soil with added grit
for extra drainage.

This type of cactus is prone to rot, so
water sparingly during the growing
season and ensure good drainage.
Feed with a balanced liquid fertiliser at
four-week intervals during the growing
season. It should bloom from a young
age if well cared for.

Matucana weberbaueri

*Syn. Echinocactus weberbaueri,
Borzicactus weberbaueri*

A rounded-to-spherical perennial
cactus which becomes columnar. It
has 25–30 ribs on the stem, creamy
white areoles, and bears dense,
golden-coloured spines in a pattern of
1–3 centrals and 25–30 radials. The
spines can be so compacted that the
plant appears to have a golden hue.
The flowers are solitary, red to orange,
long-necked and funnel shaped. They
are borne near the crown in spring
or summer.

✳ Height and Spread

Matucana weberbaueri grows to 30 cm in
height and 10 cm in diameter.

✳ Location and Temperature

Indoors, grow it in bright light in a warm
room, ideally at an average temperature
of 12°C. It prefers morning sunlight.
Outside, grow it in light shade where
the temperature remains above 10°C. It
may tolerate a short frost if it has been
kept dry.

✳ Growing Medium and Maintenance

Indoors, grow it in a mix of four parts
standard cactus or multipurpose
soil-based compost to one-part limestone
chippings. Outdoors, grow in fertile,
well-drained, humus-rich alkaline soil.

This cactus needs good drainage at all
times, and should never have its roots
standing in water. Water it in the growing
season but reduce watering during winter.
Keep it warm at all times in winter.

Opuntia pailana

A branching, rounded cactus with flattened stems and many areoles, each with several spines. It has a glaucous, silvery appearance. In common with other opuntias, it not only has normal spines, but also thin, barbed spines, named glochids. Moving the plant can result in some of these glochids becoming airborne, so due caution is required. Its flowers are large, white and funnel shaped, appearing in spring to summer. They are followed by spherical fruit.

✳ Height and Spread

This plant grows to 90 cm in height with a spread of 50 cm.

✳ Location and Temperature

Grow it in a bright, well-lit place. It suits a temperate greenhouse. If planted in a container, leave lots of room for growth which can be retarded by root constraint. Grow it outdoors in full sun where temperatures remain above 10°C (minimum 7°C). It suits a desert or arid garden.

✳ Growing Medium and Maintenance

Indoors, grow it in proprietary multipurpose or standard cactus compost. Outdoors, grow it in fertile, freely-draining soil with added humus and grit.

Water from spring to late summer, keeping the growing medium moist. Apply a balanced liquid fertiliser at monthly intervals during the growing season. Keep it dry in winter.

Oreocereus celsianus

Old Man of the Andes

Syn. Borzicactus celsianus, Cereus celsianus, Pilocereus celsianus, Oreocereus maximus

A tall, columnar cactus, which branches slowly from the base. The stems have 10–16 ribs with tubercles. Its areoles are woolly, grey and bear very sharp yellow spines in a pattern of 1–4 centrals and 7–10 radials. The spines are hidden in the long, white hairs. It bears showy pink flowers up to 9 cm long in summer.

✳ Height and Spread

It can reach a height of 3 m and a width of 10 cm.

✳ Location and Temperature

Indoors, grow it in a bright place or in a warm greenhouse. Outdoors, grow it in full sun. When it is very hot, it will need protection from the midday sun. It needs a minimum temperature of 10°C but will withstand frost down to –12°C for short periods.

✳ Growing Medium and Maintenance

Indoors, grow it in four-parts proprietary multipurpose compost or standard cactus compost to one-part limestone chippings. Outdoors, grow it in fertile, freely-draining, humus-rich, slightly alkaline (pH 7.5–8.5) soil with slow-release fertiliser added.

Water lightly between spring and summer and apply a balanced liquid fertiliser at four-weekly intervals during the growing season. Keep it dry at all other times as it will rot easily if over-watered. Care needs to be taken when handling this cactus as its spines are very sharp.

Oreocereus trollii

Old Man of the Mountain
*Syn. Cereus trollii, Borzicactus trollii,
Oreocereus bruennowii*

This is a columnar, slowly-clumping,
perennial cactus originating in the
mountains of Argentina and southern
Bolivia. It is densely covered in white
hairs, giving it a bearded appearance.
These hairs protect it from sudden
temperature changes. The stems have
many ribs and tubercles. The areoles
bear brown spines to 2 cm in length.
Mature plants bear bright red, single
flowers from the region of the stem tips.
These appear in summer and may grow
up to 4 cm in diameter.

✳ Height and Spread
It can reach a height of 60 cm with
a width of 10 cm.

✳ Location and Temperature
Indoors, grow it in a bright place or in
a warm greenhouse. Outdoors, grow
it in full sun. It prefers a minimum
temperature of 10°C, but will withstand
frost down to –7°C for short periods.

✳ Growing Medium and Maintenance
Indoors, grow *Oreocereus trollii* in four
parts proprietary multipurpose compost,
or standard cactus compost to one-part
limestone chippings. Outdoors, grow in
fertile, freely-draining, humus-rich,
slightly alkaline (pH 7.5–8.5) soil with
slow-release fertiliser added.

Water it between spring and summer
every time the compost starts drying out.
Apply a balanced liquid fertiliser at
four-weekly intervals during the growing
season. Keep it dry at all other times.
It will rot easily if watered during
the winter.

Oroya peruviana

Artichoke Cactus
Syn. Echinocactus peruvianus,
Oroya peruvian var. haumanii,
Oroya neoperuviana, Oroya subocculta

A beautiful, perennial cactus which is often grafted on to a rootstock as it is difficult to propagate. Its stems are flattened, cylindrical, bluish green and rarely branch. The stems have up to forty ribs and many notched tubercles. The areoles bear brown or yellow spines in a pattern of six centrals and 15–30 radials. The stunning, funnel-shaped flowers appear in a ring around the crown of each stem in summer and are in mixed shades of pink, usually with yellow bases. These are followed by yellow berries.

❋ Height and Spread
Oroya peruviana grows up to 30 cm high, and spreads up to 20 cm.

❋ Location and Temperature
Indoors, grow in a bright place. Outdoors, grow in full sun. This cactus is not frost hardy and needs a minimum average temperature of 10°C.

❋ Growing Medium and Maintenance
Indoors, grow it in proprietary multipurpose compost or standard cactus compost. Outdoors, grow it in freely-draining, poor, humus-rich soil that is neutral or slightly alkaline (pH 7–8).

Give it water from spring to autumn and keep it completely dry in winter. Apply half-strength balanced liquid fertiliser at six-weekly intervals during the growing season. It is a difficult plant to grow.

Parodia chrysacanthion

Golden Powder Puff

Syn. Echinocactus microspermus,
Echinocactus chrysacanthion

This beautiful cactus takes its name from
the Greek meaning 'golden spines'. It
grows a globular to columnar stem with
pale green flesh. It has up to twenty-four
spiralled, warty ribs. The crown is a mass
of thick, golden yellow wool, hence its
common name. The areoles are creamy
yellow and bear yellow spines in a
pattern of 1–2 centrals and 30–40 radials.
The bright, golden-yellow flowers are
funnel shaped and appear near the crown
from late winter to late spring. This cactus
is often slow to grow in the first year.

✳ Height and Spread

It can reach a height of 20 cm and
a spread of 10 cm.

✳ Location and Temperature

Indoors, grow it in full or bright sunlight.
Outdoors, grow it in full sun (but protect
it from midday sun), or light shade. It
requires a minimum temperature of 10°C,
but will withstand frost to –10°C for very
short periods.

✳ Growing Medium and Maintenance

Indoors, grow it in proprietary
multipurpose or standard cactus compost.
Outdoors, grow it in well-drained,
fertile soil.

Water from spring to late summer,
keeping the compost moist but not over-
wet. Apply a low nitrogen liquid fertiliser
at four-weekly intervals in the growing
season. Keep it almost dry in winter. It
will rot easily if the substrate is wet and
cold, and tends to lose its roots in winter.

Parodia haselbergii ssp. graessneri

Syn. Notocactus graessneri, Echinocactus graessneri, Brasilicactus graessneri

A globular cactus with a spherical, dark green stem, an angled, spiny crown, and 50–60 warty ribs with pronounced tubercles along their length. The stems elongate with age. The areoles are white and bear golden-yellow, or pale brown to white spines in the pattern of 6 centrals and 50–60 radials. Pale yellow-green, funnel-shaped flowers are produced in spring. These can be 2.5 cm across and last for several weeks.

✳ Height and Spread

This cacti grows to a height of 12 cm, with a diameter up to 8 cm.

✳ Location and Temperature

Indoors, grow it in bright filtered, or full, light. Outdoors, grow it in light shade or partial sun. It should be kept at an average minimum temperature of 10°C, and does not like to become too hot. It is frost tender but will withstand occasional frost.

✳ Growing Medium and Maintenance

Indoors, grow it in standard cactus compost, or soil-based multipurpose compost, with a layer of grit at the top. Outdoors, grow it in fertile, well-drained soil.

Water from spring to summer to keep the compost just damp, but ensure excess water drains away freely. It will rot easily if the soil is wet and cold, and tends to lose its roots in winter. Apply a liquid low nitrogen fertiliser at six-weekly intervals during the growing season.

Parodia magnifica

Balloon Cactus

Syn. Notocactus magnificus, Eriocactus magnificus

An intriguing spherical, or short columnar, clustering cactus with 11–15 marked ribs with grey-green flesh. Its stems are up to 12 cm in diameter and the ribs bear small, grey, velvety areoles with golden to grey, hairy spines in a pattern of twelve longer centrals and 12–15 radials. Its flowers are bright yellow, funnel shaped and bloom in late spring. They can grow up to 3 cm across.

✳ Height and Spread

Parodia magnifica grows up to 15 cm high. The clusters can reach 50 cm in diameter, with each individual head being up to 12 cm across.

✳ Location and Temperature

Indoors, grow in airy, bright conditions in full sunlight. Outdoors, grow in light shade to full sun, it suits a desert garden. Some shade is needed inside and outside at the hottest times of the year. It requires an average temperature of 10°C, but will tolerate some frost to –7°C for short periods.

✳ Growing Medium and Maintenance

Indoors, grow it in proprietary multipurpose or standard cactus compost. Outdoors, grow it in free-draining, fertile soil.

Water regularly in summer and keep it almost dry in winter. It will rot easily if the growing medium stays wet or cold, and tends to lose its roots in winter.

Parodia mammulosa ssp. submammulosa

Tom Thumb

Syn. Notocactus submammulosus,
Echinocactus submammulosus var.
submammulosus, Ritterocactus
mammulosus ssp. submammulosus

A globular to cylindrical cactus with dark
green stems and a woolly crown. The
stems have 12–20 ribs with pronounced,
warty tubercles. Areoles are white and
bear white-grey spines in a pattern of
2–4 longer centrals and 6–25 radials. The
pale golden-yellow flowers have darker
yellow inner parts and bright red stigmas.
They are funnel shaped, up to 5 cm
across and are produced in summer.

✳ Height and Spread

Parodia mammulosa
grows to 13 cm high
and 6 cm across.

✳ Location and Temperature

Indoors, grow it in bright filtered light. It
should be kept at a minimum average
temperature of 10°C. In colder climates,
a warm greenhouse is more suitable.
Outdoors, grow it in partial shade. It
should do well in a desert garden, but
is not frost hardy.

✳ Growing Medium and Maintenance

Indoors, grow it in proprietary
multipurpose or standard cactus compost.
The compost should be open and not
compacted. Outdoors, grow it
in well-drained, fertile soil.

Water Tom Thumb regularly in summer
and keep it almost dry in winter. It will
rot easily if the soil is wet and cold, and
tends to lose its roots in winter.

Rebutia marsoneri 'krainziana'

Hedgehog Cactus
Syn. Rebutia krainziana,
Rebutia calliantha var. krainziana,
Rebutia wessneriana var. krainziana

A perennial, clustering dwarf cactus which originates at high altitudes (around 4000 m) in Bolivia and northwest Argentina. It has depressed, spherical, warty stems and bright green flesh. The stems have 20 or more spiral ribs. The white areoles are close together and bear 8–12 spines. It is a highly desirable plant as it blooms easily, bearing bright red, relatively large flowers up to 3.5 cm across which originate near the base of the stems in summer.

❋ Height and Spread
It grows up to 10 cm high and has a spread up to 7 cm.

❋ Location and Temperature
Indoors, grow it in full light, but not too much direct sunlight, and with low humidity. It is suited to a bright windowsill or temperate greenhouse. Outdoors, grow it in full sun or light shade. This cactus requires an average minimum temperature of 8°C and is not frost tolerant.

❋ Growing Medium and Maintenance
Indoors, grow it in proprietary multipurpose compost, or standard cactus compost. Outdoors, grow it in gritty, fairly fertile, slightly acidic soil that is free draining. Water from spring to summer, allowing the compost to dry between waterings, and apply a liquid balanced fertiliser at eight-week intervals. Keep it dry at other times of the year.

Rhipsalis baccifera

Mistletoe Cactus
Syn. Rhipsalis heptagona,
Cassyta baccifera, Rhipsalis dichotoma,
Hariota fascicilata, Cactus caripensis

An epiphytic, hanging forest cactus which
has aerial roots and very fine (5 mm
thick), cylindrical, mid-green stems. Its
tiny areoles are spineless and produce
small clusters of funnel-shaped white
flowers from winter to spring. Its common
name comes from the white berries that
appear after flowering.

✳ Height and Spread

Its hanging stems grow to 1.8 m in length
and the plant reaches 60 cm in width.

✳ Location and Temperature

Indoors, ensure high humidity during
the growing season. It will also suit a
conservatory or warm greenhouse.
Outdoors, grow in an open site with a
minimum temperature of 7°C and
protection on the coldest nights.

✳ Growing Medium and Maintenance

Indoors, grow it in epiphytic compost
or soil-based, porous multipurpose
compost with added sterile leaf mould or
peat. Outdoors, grow in soil that is rich in
organic matter.

Mist this cactus daily in summer and
water it generously in the growing
season, especially when in flower. Make
sure the water can drain away freely.
Apply a liquid balanced fertiliser at
six-weekly intervals. Keep it just moist
at all other times.

Schlumbergera 'Thor Brita'

Christmas Cacti, S. 'Limelight Dancer'

This perennial cactus is erect when young, and only later develops its pendular habit. It has fleshy, green stems divided into several segments, each with distinctive, notched edges which give them a leaf-like appearance. The areoles bear a few bristle-like spines and appear close to the tips of stems where they produce trumpet-shaped flowers in late winter or early spring. The white blooms appear more readily when days are short, which is why this cactus flowers around Christmas time in temperate climates. S. 'Limelight Dancer' (pictured) is a popular and similar variety of Christmas cacti and has pale flowers with a pink tube inside.

☀ Height and Spread

It grows up to 90 cm in diameter, with stems up to 60 cm long.

☀ Location and Temperature

It can be grown in a warm greenhouse, or as a potted plant, in indirect but bright light. It is also suited to a basket where its stems can overhang the edges. It can be grown outside in warmer areas but needs protection from rain. In all cases, avoid direct sun in summer, and shelter from draughts indoors and strong winds outdoors. It needs a minimum average temperature of 12°C and is not frost tolerant.

☀ Growing Medium and Maintenance

Grow it indoors in epiphytic compost (pH6), or outdoors in humus-rich, moisture-retentive, but well-drained soil with added grit and leaf mould.

Apply high-potash liquid fertiliser at two-weekly intervals when growing, to encourage blooms. It requires a rest period from February to April, then should be treated normally, watering when the compost dries out. From October, when buds form, increase the temperature and water more frequently. Re-pot it once it has out-grown its pot, usually after 3–4 years.

Thelocactus tulensis ssp. matudae

Syn. Thelocactus matudae, Thelocactus buekii ssp. matudae

Thelocactus tulensis matudae is a solitary cactus with a deep-green stem, that has a whitish tinge, and prominent tubercles which reach 2.5 cm in length. The white areoles bear grey spines up to 2 cm in length in a pattern of 3–7 centrals and 7–12 radials. The magnificent, creamy white flowers have brown stripes and appear in early summer. They can be up to 8 cm across.

✳ Height and Spread

It grows up to 22 cm high and spreads up to 15 cm.

✳ Location and Temperature

Indoors, grow it in full light and with low humidity on a brightly-lit windowsill or in a cool or temperate greenhouse. Outdoors, grow it in full sun. It needs a minimum temperature of 7°C and does not tolerate frost.

✳ Growing Medium and Maintenance

Indoors, grow it in proprietary multipurpose compost or standard cactus compost. Outdoors, grow it in gritty, poor, freely-draining soil. Water from spring to early autumn and keep it dry at other times. It requires very little fertiliser, so only feed it three or four times in the growing season if growth seems slow.

Turbinicarpus schmiedickeanus ssp. schwarzii

Syn. Pediocactus schmiedickeanus var. schwarzii, Neolloydia schmiedickeanus var. schwarzii

A usually solitary, occasionally clumping, flattened, very small cactus. It has a pale green, rounded stem with 2–12 ribs and flattened angular tubercles which bear 1–3 soft, grey, curved spines. It is a very slow-growing cactus. The flowers are funnel shaped, cream with a pale pink central stripe on each petal, and appear in spring.

✳ Height and Spread
It grows to 2 cm in height with a spread of up to 5 cm.

✳ Location and Temperature
Indoors, grow it in full light on a draught-free windowsill. Outdoors, grow it in full sun. Minimum temperature of 12°C.

✳ Growing Medium and Maintenance
Indoors, grow it in proprietary multipurpose or standard cactus compost. Outdoors, grow it in well-drained, moderately fertile, humus-rich soil. Water this cactus from mid-spring to autumn, never allowing it to stand in water. Feed with a dilute, balanced liquid fertiliser at four-weekly intervals.

Propagation

While many may prefer to buy established plants, it is possible to propagate cacti. The following is a general guide to the key methods.

✳ Seed

The most common way to propagate cacti is through seed. Some species of cacti are self-fertile, which means they can pollinate themselves. To ensure self-pollination, it is best to cover their flowers with a plastic bag which prevents insects cross-pollinating the plants.

By gently tapping the bag, pollen is released, thus allowing self-pollination to occur. However, many cacti are not self-fertile and require pollen from another plant of the same species in order to produce seeds. In this case, pollination can be achieved by using a small paintbrush to lift the pollen gently from the anther of one plant and to transfer it to the stigma of another.

More usually, seeds are bought in packets from commercial stockists. Sow seeds in trays or in individual pots depending on the species of cactus and the size of the seed. Choose a moist, clean compost (which can be the same as used for larger plants), but sieve it to remove larger particles. Place or sprinkle the seeds on the surface and cover them with a thin layer of coarse grit.

Most seeds will germinate at a temperature of about 21°C. Increasing the temperature slightly at nightfall will improve germination. Keep the atmosphere humid while the seeds germinate. This may be done by sealing the pots with plastic bags or covering seed trays with glass.

Once the seeds have germinated they can be introduced to light and more air, but not direct sunlight at this stage. Seedlings should never be allowed to dry out completely, and damping off (a fungal infection caused by excessive moisture) can be prevented by using a copper fungicide solution.

✳ Cuttings

Many cacti are easily propagated from cuttings. These cuttings are susceptible to fungal infections so the surfaces must be kept clean, with a callous permitted to form before they are placed in soil. This can take from a day to a week or two depending on the surface area of the cut.

In most cases, stem or root cuttings are taken at a narrow point to minimise the cut area. The cuttings should be placed lightly in compost: some specimens benefit from gentle bottom heat at this stage.

Some clumping cacti form roots from stems while on the parent plant, and these can be cut off and quickly potted up. Hormone rooting powder may be useful in some cases.

✳ Flat Grafting

Grafting plants onto vigorous rootstock is a popular method of propagating cacti. It can also be used to keep cristate forms away from the soil to avoid rotting, and to force some species to produce offsets which are then used to produce new plants. It is also used to propagate interesting genetic mutations – those lacking chlorophyll, for example – and to encourage slow-growing species to flower early. Plants commonly used for grafts are *Echinopsis* and *Trichocereus*.

Use a sharp knife to cut the top of the rootstock plant, and bevel the surface so it does not become concave when dry. Cut the bottom off the scion (the shoot) and press the two cut edges together, ensuring the vascular bundles of each plant line up. Hold the edges together using elastic bands or clips and weights, and place the plant in a warm place out of direct sunlight and in a slightly humid atmosphere.

In a couple of weeks, the union should be strong enough for the pressure to be removed. Other grafting methods, such as side grafting and apical wedge grafting, can also be successful.

✳ Pad Sections

Many cacti can be propagated by taking pads from the parent plant. A pad is cut using a sharp knife and a cut is made straight across the joint. The cutting is allowed to dry for 48 hours and is then inserted into a pot containing equal parts of fine peat substitute and sharp grit or sand. After rooting, pot on into standard cactus compost.

✳ Stem Sections

Cut a mature cactus stem into 8 cm sections and insert them into compost to root.

✳ Offsets

Many clump-forming cacti can be propagated from offsets early in the growing season. Scrape away the soil to reveal the base of the offset and carefully cut it from the parent plant. Treat the wound with fungicide and leave it to form a callous.

Pot up the offsets as soon as possible and water them lightly. Keep the offsets in semi-shade for two weeks at a temperature of 15ºC. Water them again lightly after the first week. Once new growth starts, they should be potted into the appropriate growing medium and grown as normal.

Some species form offsetting tubers which should be detached gently, the wounds treated with fungicide, and the tubers inserted into potting compost if they have roots, or a mix of sand and fine peat substitute in equal parts if the roots are absent. Top dress with a 5 mm layer of grit and leave them to dry for several days.

☀ Root Division

Many branching cacti can be propagated by dividing the roots, carefully separating the rootstock into sections and re-potting separately.

☀ Pollination and Cross-breeding across Groups

Cross-pollination between varieties can occur naturally if a collection of cacti are grown. The resulting hybrids are sometimes worth keeping, but usually plants are weak and have few desirable qualities.

Selected hybrids can be created between varieties of the same species. Choose plants that have desirable characteristics and, just before the anthers swell or ripen, cover the flowers with a small, loosely-tied paper bag. This prevents unwanted insect pollination.

Using a small, soft brush, transfer the pollen from the anthers of one plant to the stigmas of another. Re-cover the pollinated flower for a couple of days, then wait.

Many hybrids fail, but sometimes a superb specimen with desirable qualities from both parents results. Commercially, cross-pollination is used to produce new varieties of cacti with some success.

Pests and Diseases

Cacti, like most plants, are susceptible to several pests and diseases. The following examples are some of the most common.

✳ Mealy Bug

Woolly aphids (*Pseudococcus spp.*), a variety of mealy bug, can kill even large plants quickly and are the most common pest of cacti. They are 1–3 mm long and are recognised as white, woolly patches on the plant. They can remain dormant for long periods, hidden in axils, hair or amongst spines.

Some strains are resistant to chemicals, but strong jets of water can wash away the pests, and removing them by hand is also effective. Cotton buds soaked in methylated spirit will kill them but can damage the plant.

It is easier to try to and avoid the introduction of mealy bugs in the first place by quarantining new plants and promptly dealing with the first signs of any infection. Good hygiene is important as mealy bugs hide under dead vegetation and old flowers.

Some mealy bugs attack the roots (Root Mealy Bug, *Rhizoecus spp.*). These are not usually noticed until the damage has been done, so regularly lift and check plants. If a plant suddenly becomes sick, lift it from its pot and check its roots for white tufts. Wash the roots in a jet of water or systemic insecticide, dry them, and re-pot the plant in fresh soil.

✳ Red Spider Mites

These are minute but can do a lot of damage. Look for webbing and brown scarring on the plants. Chemicals based on butoxycarboxim can control these pests. They are encouraged by a lack of ventilation and hot, dry conditions, so keep the growing area well ventilated and slightly humid.

Scale Insects

Opuntias, in particular, seem prone to this pest which is seen as tough scales clinging to the stems. Direct spraying is not very effective but systemic insecticides appear to work, as does hand removal.

Western Flower Thrips

A relatively new pest to cacti, this fast-moving insect is seen on the flowers. It causes the blooms to distort and reduces their fertility. Blue-coloured sticky tape makes an effective trap.

Slugs and Snails

These pests are particularly attracted to succulent, juicy, young cacti. Keep greenhouses clean, and clear of places for them to hide. Hand removal is most successful but needs to be done at night when they are most active. Slug bait can be used in extreme cases.

Ants

Ants do little harm to cacti but can introduce mealy bugs or other aphids, so should be controlled by regularly disturbing their nests or, if the problem is severe, by using powdered insecticide.

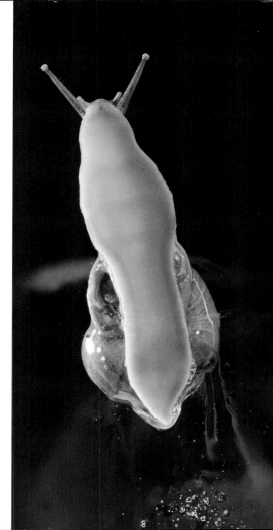

☀ Leaf-cutter Bees

Leaf-cutter bees can damage the tuberous roots of cacti as they tunnel through to the soil to make their nests. They seem particularly attracted to plants kept in hanging baskets. To prevent these pests from becoming a problem, re-pot the plants, removing any nests.

☀ Sciarid Flies

The grubs of these tiny flies can damage young seedlings and the problem usually occurs in damp, peat-based composts. Yellow, sticky insecticidal strips are effective in trapping the adults, so breaking the breeding cycle.

☀ Eelworms or Nematodes

Usually prevalent in warmer climates, the large, egg-carrying cysts of these pests cause stunted growth in cacti. The treatment is to immerse the plant in water at 50°C for twenty minutes. Re-pot using fresh soil.

☀ Greenfly

Rarely a problem, but they do occasionally attack the flowers of cacti. Hand removal, spraying with soapy water, or simply removing the flower heads are all effective.

☀ Rotting

Fungal and bacterial infections of the roots are one of the most common causes of failure in cacti. Generally, healthy plants can resist infections. However, damage from insects, or physical damage to the plant, can result in an attack. A major cause of rot is through bacteria entering the plant via roots which have died through poor aeration or over-watering.

The best way to avoid problems is through good horticultural practice and the prevention of the damp conditions in which fungi thrive. If rot is spotted early, try to cut out the diseased tissue with a knife previously cleaned in alcohol.

Fungicidal chemicals provide some protection but are not effective against all fungi. Copper-based fungicide is effective against damping off (fungal infection caused by excessive moisture), which mainly affects young plants and seedlings.

☀ Deficiency Diseases

Plants lacking essential minerals will not grow well. It may not be simply that the soil lacks these essentials, but that the plants cannot obtain them – this is often due to a build up of minerals from tap water which eventually makes the soil too alkaline. It is a good idea to check the water you use on your plants and, if necessary, add dihydrogen phosphate, which increases acidity and provides essential minerals. If your local rainwater is clean, it is probably the best thing to use to water your cacti.

Peat-based composts are more prone to deficiencies than others. If a plant looks yellow, or is slow to grow, try fresh compost. If using local soil, check to see if there is a known deficiency and, if necessary, add appropriate supplements.

Conclusion

These characterful, prickly plants can provide a constant source of interest – whether you are looking for unusual form, glorious flowers, a uniform collection, an eclectic group or just a solitary plant, there's bound to be a cactus that will suit your taste.

If you provide its basic needs – the right situation, light, temperature and a little food and water now and then – your cactus should reward you with healthy growth, regular flowering and year-round interest.